P9-BYD-938

Walk The Talk is both an inspiration and a warning. It sends a timeless message to all businesses: Companies are more than buildings, balance sheets, and bottom lines—people and their values are the resources that produce lasting competitive advantage.

—Frank K. Sonnenberg, President,
RMI Marketing & Advertising
and author of *Marketing to Win*

Several years ago in *The Goal*, Eli Goldratt used fiction to deliver some profound thoughts about managing a manufacturing operation. Its message has remained fresh in my mind largely because of the exciting fashion in which it was presented. Harvey and Lucia have now joined the club. *Walk The Talk* has a powerful message that, because of its fascinating allegorical presentation, will become permanently imbedded in readers' minds. It's must reading for every executive who wants to be effective in the '90s.

—William J. Altier, CMC
President, Princeton Associates

In every seminar I've given in the last four years, someone always mentions the need for managers to 'walk their talk'—finally, a book that teaches in a straight-forward way what we've all needed for years. Congratulations.

—Peter Grazier, President
Teambuilding, Inc.

How does our corporate behavior match our values? Not an easy subject in anyone's book. *Walk The Talk* takes on a difficult challenge and succeeds. I recommend it highly.

—Al Berstein
Co-author of *Dinosaur Brains* and *Neanderthals at Work*

Walk the Talk

. . . And Get the Results You Want

Eric L. Harvey
Alexander D. Lucia

Published by: Treeview Publishing, a subsidiary of
Performance Systems Corporation
2925 LBJ Freeway, Suite 201
Dallas, Texas 75234

Treeview Publishing books may be purchased for educational, business, or sales promotional use. For information please write:
Performance Systems Corporation
2925 LBJ Freeway, Suite 201
Dallas, Texas 75234

Library of Congress Cataloging-in-Publication Data
Harvey, Eric L.
Walk the Talk: and get the results you want /
Eric Harvey and Alexander Lucia.—1st ed
LCCN: 93-143650
ISBN 1-885228-00-7
1. Management. I. Lucia, Alexander. II. Title
HD

First Edition

All characters, companies and events portrayed in this book are fictitious. Any resemblance to actual people, names, companies, and events is purely coincidental.

Printed in the United States of America
10 9 8 7 6 5

Foreword

by Ken Blanchard

My wife Marjorie and I have long preached the value of walking your talk. It seemed so much easier a decade ago when we were just starting a seminar business. But as business at Blanchard Training & Development has grown greatly over the past ten years, we have discovered how hard it is to practice daily what we preach.

We all struggle with the same basic issues in business: how to get our group to perform like a team; how to hire, retain and manage productive people; how to be more profitable; and how to be in sync with our mission, vision and values.

Surely there exists a little Don Quixote in us all. In our corporate lives we seek solutions to the challenges of competition, downsizing, delegation, quality and corporate integrity. On occasion, something comes along that clears our minds and lights our paths. Someone looks anew at the ordinary and transforms it into the extraordinary.

Eric Harvey and Al Lucia have done just that with their masterful little book, *Walk the Talk*. Don't jump to conclusions when you read the title. Don't assume you already understand the concept. As a veteran proponent of the virtues of empowerment, integrity, and quality, I found *Walk the Talk* to be an "ah-ha" experience. It helped me and Marjorie to put all our concerns for quality and equity in a valuable new perspective.

Harvey and Lucia have used a magical allegory to translate difficult concepts and corporate contradictions into personal convictions. Through the character of Clarence, a delightfully mysterious janitor, they invite you into the process of personal discovery so gently that you volunteer for the assignment.

So much has been written and spoken about "walking the talk" and with good reason. I firmly believe that it is the very essence of what today's management must adopt as the credo of choice, so I wanted this book to live up to its title. It does! It is a "fast read," the lively episode lasts roughly an hour. And in the pages of this clever story lie great insights. Harvey and Lucia have shown us how to blend values and ideals into daily practice.

Walk the Talk asks us to look inside—inside ourselves and inside the workings of our organizations. It invites us to slow down and take stock of our resources. We are challenged to become cultivators of the rich resource of people, their fertile minds and hidden talents. It espouses honesty and integrity but goes even deeper—calling us to be better stewards of both our corporate and individual lives.

Walk the Talk is a book about living out our convictions and dealing with our contradictions. Whether the deed or the company is large or small, there is little that goes unnoticed.

Delegating, empowering, and turning your beliefs into practice are all integral to walking the talk. I invite you to take your own journey through the pages of *Walk the Talk* and discover its value for your own life.

Ken Blanchard, co-author of the One Minute Manager *library, is chairman of Blanchard Training & Development in Escondido, California.*

Introduction

Acting in accord with our beliefs and values is one of the greatest challenges that each of us faces every day. It's true in all aspects of life, from family and religion to sports and politics—and it's especially true in business.

Most organizations today *talk* a good management game. Mission statements and operating beliefs can be found everywhere from corporate lobbies and conference rooms to employee handbooks and annual reports. These public displays of good intention are reminders of what we stand for, what we are about. But the true worth of beliefs and values comes from the extent to which they are practiced rather than merely professed.

Saying the right words is the easy part. Walking the talk and doing the right things is the tough challenge.

Walk the Talk is intended to help you understand and meet that challenge. As you read, you'll share the experiences of a new CEO named Bill Elby and his very special teacher—a janitor named Clarence. You'll travel with them as they confirm what so many successful people have taught us over the years:

When you walk like you talk,
you get the results you want.

Eric Harvey
Al Lucia

Acknowledgement

We express our appreciation to the staff at Performance Systems for contributing to an environment where good ideas can "walk in" at any time.

Walk the Talk is a book about the inherent worth of people. Throughout this project, we have learned much about commitment, cooperation, and unselfish dedication. These priceless qualities are integral to the success of any substantive endeavor. So from the bottom of our hearts, thank you, Steve Ventura! We could not have done it without you.

Eric & Al

The Walking Teeth

It's amazing what you can learn from a creative employee and a cute trinket!

One day we came to work and found on each of our desks a walking teeth wind-up toy. These toys were gifts from a member of our staff who realized their significance long before we did.

We played with those teeth endlessly—watching them chatter as they marched back and forth. They continued to be nothing more than a source of humorous pleasure until it finally occurred to us that these simple toys convey a profound message.

And so we've adopted the teeth as the visual symbol of our theme. We hope that whenever you see them throughout this book, you'll be reminded of how important it is for all of us to *walk the talk.*

Contents

The Rehearsal

Bill Elby had never been more anxious.

Tomorrow he would deliver his first "state of the company" address to employees since becoming chief executive of Treeview Industries one year ago.

He had spent the past week struggling to find just the right words and prove correct the friend who said, "Don't worry, something always comes to you."

Leaving nothing to chance, he had come to the empty company auditorium to practice his prepared speech one final time.

After arranging his notes on the podium, Bill gazed briefly at the empty seats in front of him, took a deep breath, and began:

> *"Fellow Treeview employees, I appreciate the opportunity to speak to you today about our business. It truly is my pleasure to address such a fine group of people. As you know, our financial picture could be much better than it is. Nevertheless, we have made several significant accomplishments during this past year. We . . ."*

He continued—working his way through the list of achievements, a somewhat dismal financial report, and a review of a planned reorganization that he hoped would be the key to Treeview's future prosperity.

Suddenly a noise from the back of the auditorium brought the rehearsal to an abrupt halt.

"Who's there?" asked Bill.

"It's just me, Clarence, the janitor," came a response from the dark. "I'm supposed to clean this place up."

"Go right ahead, Clarence," said Bill. "I'm Bill Elby. I'm just practicing my speech for tomorrow."

"Yes sir, I know who you are," replied Clarence. "You just keep on practicing. You won't bother me a bit."

"That's terrific," chuckled the CEO, who found it refreshing to meet someone so apparently *under*whelmed by his presence.

After finding his place, Bill continued:

"Despite our current financial position, I am optimistic about the future. You only have to review our corporate values and philosophies to know that we're the kind of organization that's destined to be successful. We believe that our employees are our most valuable resource and that quality is our primary objective. We believe in working together to solve problems. We believe in decision making at the lowest possible level. And, we believe in trust, mutual respect, and a partnership approach to doing business."

By now, Clarence had worked his way forward from the darkness into the light. Bill could clearly see a smile on the weathered yet warm face of this man he didn't recognize. Wondering if that broad smile was a response to his speech, Bill engaged his one-person audience.

"Were you listening to what I was saying, Clarence?"

"Yes, sir, I sure was," answered the janitor.

"What do you think?" continued the CEO. "About that last part I mean."

"Good words."

"You're right!" spouted Bill. "Those are our values, and they *are* good words."

"Words to live by?" probed the janitor politely.

"Absolutely," answered Bill. "Words to live by. But why do you ask?"

"Well," replied Clarence, removing his cap and wiping the perspiration from his face and neck, "I've been around here darn near forever. I've cleaned up after a lot of folks who've come and gone over the years, and I've heard lots of good words just like those."

"That's because they're important," said Bill. "That's why we talk about them, and why we've put them in our company publications and posted them all over the place."

"I understand," responded Clarence. "But it seems to me that words to live by are just words, unless you live by them. You have to *walk* the talk."

"Those are good words, too," said Bill. "Very profound for . . ."

"For an old janitor?" interrupted Clarence.

"Yes," said Bill, "profound for a janitor."

"Well, believe it or not," said Clarence, revealing a somewhat feisty side to his personality, "I don't check in my brains when I check out my brooms."

"I didn't intend that as a put-down. It's just that you're probably pretty isolated from what we do around here every day."

"I think you'd be surprised what you can pick up when you pick up. That's a janitor joke!" laughed Clarence. "Anyway, I know a lot about what goes on here. Maybe more than you might think."

"I'll bet you do," replied Bill, in an attempt to appease the old man with a few more seconds of attention. "Tell me, what do you mean by the words 'walk the talk'?"

Words to live by
are just words,
unless you live
by them.
You have to
walk the talk.

"Well," said Clarence, "let's see. Have you ever made a promise you didn't keep?"

"Of course! Everyone, at one time or another, has had a good intention they didn't deliver on."

"What do you suppose happens when we don't deliver on something we've promised?" asked Clarence.

"Obviously, we lose trust and credibility. If it happens too many times, our promises become meaningless."

"That's what I think, too," said Clarence. "And that's why we have to walk the talk. Those good words you spoke earlier are like promises. People read and hear them, and then they expect the promises to be kept. But, if what they actually see is different than what they hear and read, there's a problem. Like my grandpa used to say, 'when you break a promise, more than the promise gets broken.'"

Looking somewhat troubled, Bill asked, "Are you saying we don't walk our talk here at Treeview?"

"Sometimes folks do," answered Clarence, "and sometimes they don't. But one thing's for sure—business seems to run a lot smoother around here when people DO!"

"So, you've seen what happens when we walk the talk . . . and when we don't?" asked Bill.

"Yes sir, I sure have."

Like most CEO's, Bill was not in the habit of seeking advice from janitors. But somehow this situation was different. As he looked into the eyes of the old janitor, Bill could tell there was more to this man than met the eye. He sensed an indefinable something that tempered his sarcastic inclinations and compelled him to probe deeper. "I suppose you can tell me about some of those examples?"

"Heck, I can do better than that," said Clarence. "If you have a few minutes, I can *show* you."

"Actually, I'm very busy right now," said Bill, glancing at his watch. "I really don't have the time to go anywhere. I've got to work on my speech."

"I think what I have to show you will *help* your speech," suggested the janitor. "Considering how you've been struggling with that rascal all week, what do you really have to lose?"

"How did you know I've had a tough time with the speech?" asked the CEO, whose curiosity was now peaking.

"Like I said earlier," answered Clarence, "I just might know more than you think!"

"Apparently so," Bill thought to himself.

"I bet a walk would do you good," continued Clarence. "Why don't you come with me?"

"Well," replied Bill, reluctantly, "all right. I suppose I don't have much to lose. But only for a few minutes. I'm short on time."

"It won't take long," assured Clarence.

Just then, Bill heard a faint repetitious chime. "What's that?" he asked.

"Just my watch," answered the janitor, as he pulled a small, gold pocket watch from his right pants pocket. After opening the lid and checking the watch face, Clarence continued. "It's time we took that walk."

Bill slowly followed Clarence to a set of doors at the rear of the auditorium. As they approached, the doors opened, revealing an almost blinding white light on the other side. Shielding his eyes, Bill recognized an elevator interior.

"I didn't know this was here," he said.

"Not many people do," responded Clarence with an assuring grin. "Watch your step."

Looking at the control panel, Bill quickly discovered that this was no ordinary elevator. "What's this?" he asked, as he pointed to the panel. "Where are the floor numbers?"

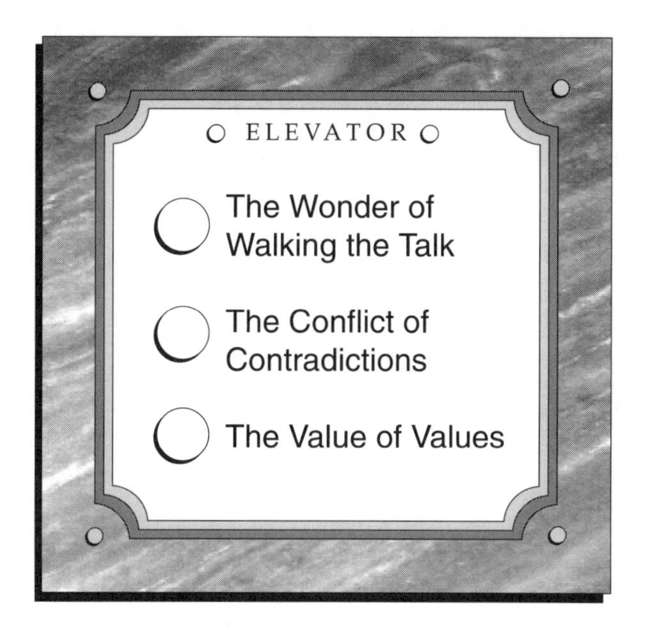

"We don't need any numbers. Those buttons will get us to where we're going."

"What's going on here, Clarence?" asked Bill. "This is not your average elevator, and it's obvious that you're not an average janitor!"

"There's nothing special about me," responded Clarence. "But this elevator is very special. It will show you everything you need to know about walking the talk. Just push that first button and see for yourself."

"This is crazy. But now I've got to know where this thing goes," muttered Bill, as he reached for the top button labeled: The Wonder of Walking The Talk.

Clarence gently grabbed Bill's arm to stop him. "Why don't we start at the bottom and work our way up," suggested the janitor with a friendly gleam.

"For some strange reason," thought the CEO, now looking into Clarence's twinkling eyes, "I trust this little man. He knows something, and I must find out what it is."

Then, following the janitor's suggestion, Bill pushed the bottom button, The Value of Values, and the elevator doors closed.

The Value of Values

The elevator doors seemed to reopen, as quickly as they had closed, into a small square room with no windows or doors. The space was stark white, and its only contents were a huge circular vault door on the back wall and a desk occupied by an elderly man wearing a security uniform.

"I don't recognize this place," said Bill. "Where are we?"

"This is where we find out about the *value of values,*" answered Clarence with a smile. "This is where our journey begins."

Exiting the elevator, Bill immediately began searching the room for clues that might explain why he was here and what this janitor, who seemed to influence him so easily, really knew.

"What's that?" asked the CEO, as he pointed to the vault.

"A vault," answered Clarence.

"I know *that*!" replied Bill. "What's *in* it?"

"Valuables," said Clarence. "That's the vault where the company valuables are kept. Valuables are too valuable to just be left lying around. Don't you agree?"

"I guess," responded Bill, not wanting to admit he had no idea what the janitor was talking about or that Treeview even had such a vault. "So who's the guy behind the desk?"

"That's the old guard," answered Clarence. "He's been around here even longer than me."

"What exactly does he do?"

"He watches over the vault and keeps people from taking the valuables out. He's been doing the same thing for the last forty years. That old guard is pretty set in his ways."

"Whatever!" snapped the CEO who was quickly moving from a state of curiosity to one of annoyance. "Look, Clarence, I've come to this room, and I've seen the guard and the vault door. So what's the point?"

"I was just about to get to that," replied Clarence with one of his reassuring smiles. "The point isn't the guard or the door. The point is what's *behind* the door. Let's go see for ourselves."

Clarence signaled Bill to follow him to the back of the room. As they approached the vault door, Bill asked, "How are we going to get in there? It looks to me like the vault is locked."

"All you have to do is dial the combination and open it up," answered the janitor.

"What combination?" questioned Bill. "And what about the guard?"

"Don't worry about the old guard. Most of the time you can get around him when he isn't looking. Besides, you *are* the boss. You can get in here any time you want. As for the combination—it's going to be in your speech."

"What are you talking about?" challenged Bill.

"I think this will be a lot clearer in just a bit, Mr. Elby. For now, why don't you just dial in the date you'll be giving that speech."

As he reached for the combination dial, Bill began to question his own sanity. "What am I doing?" he asked himself. "I've followed this old man I don't even know. And now, I'm trying to open a vault I've never seen before with a combination that just happens to be tomorrow's date."

"It's OK," assured Clarence with a wink and a nod. "Go ahead."

"What the heck," responded the CEO, "as long as I'm here. Let's see, the speech is tomorrow, February fifteenth. I guess that would be two right, fifteen left, and right ninety . . ."

"That's it," confirmed Clarence.

Bill dialed the numbers and pulled down on the locking lever. To his amazement, the door opened a few inches, and the two men were greeted by the sound and smell of escaping musty air.

"It worked!" exclaimed the CEO.

"Well done!" replied Clarence. "Now, let's see what's inside."

Bill slowly opened the door, which he found to be as heavy as it was big. Looking inside, he saw cabinets, shelves and tables.

"This is just a vault!" said the president with obvious disappointment.

"Were you expecting something else?" inquired Clarence.

"Considering what I've seen so far—you, the elevator, and this room—I guess an actual vault was the *last* thing I expected to find." Bill paused for a moment and then said, "Well, let's go in and see whatever it is we're here to see."

"I'm right behind you," said Clarence as he followed the CEO through the doorway.

"Boy, the air sure is stale in here," said Bill, as he moved to the middle of the vault.

"Yeah, it is stale," echoed Clarence. "The only time you get fresh air in here is when somebody opens the door. Guess that doesn't happen often enough."

As Clarence was talking, Bill began to survey the vault interior. On one shelf, he noticed several boxes labeled "Annual Reports That Mention Values." Another shelf was occupied by a stack of the Treeview value statements in beautiful wooden frames. On the floor in the corner was a box marked "Values Sections For Employee Handbooks."

Bill's attention finally focused on a table in the middle of the vault. Something was on top of that table, but it was covered by a cloth tarp.

"I wonder what this is?" he thought to himself, as he lifted the corner of the tarp for a quick peek. His eyes widened when he saw what was underneath.

"Holy smoke!" shouted Bill as he pulled the tarp completely off the table. "Look at this!"

Sitting in the middle of the table was a stack of yellow metal bars.

"So you found what we came here to see," said Clarence.

"If this is what I think it is," said the president, "our company's troubles are over."

"What do you think it is?" asked the janitor.

"Gold!" exclaimed Bill. "This is gold . . . and it must be worth a fortune."

"Yes sir," confirmed Clarence, "it's worth a fortune all right. Why don't you take a closer look at that fortune."

Following the janitor's suggestion, Bill bent down to examine the bars and discovered that each was inscribed across the top. He read the first inscription aloud: "We believe that our employees are our most important resource." Then he read the second: "We believe that quality is our primary objective;" and the third: "We believe in working together to solve problems."

"Sound familiar?" inquired Clarence.

"Of course they sound familiar," answered Bill. "These are the Treeview value statements. They're the very same ones we have hanging in our offices—the same ones I'm using in my speech."

"I knew you'd recognize them."

"But where did these bars come from?"

"The best I can figure," offered Clarence, "they came from all the people who work here."

"I don't understand."

"Maybe I can make it clearer by asking *you* a question," proposed the janitor. "Do you believe that there's a little gold inside everyone?"

"Sure I do!" said Bill. "I wouldn't be much of a person if I didn't believe that."

"So what do you suppose that gold is?"

Bill thought for a moment while looking at the bars, and then responded. "Values?"

"Values!" confirmed Clarence.

"So you're saying that values are the gold that's in each of us. They're the real fortune of our organization."

Values are the gold
that's in each of us.

They're the real fortune
of our organization.

"Sounds like *you're* saying that," replied Clarence, "and I think you must have known it all along. After all, you did talk about values in your speech."

"Yes, I did include our values in the speech," agreed the CEO, "because I knew they were important. But I must admit that I never really saw them as a *fortune* until now."

"Great!" exclaimed Clarence. "See, we've learned something already."

"Maybe so," replied Bill, "but there's one thing that really bothers me."

"What's that?" asked Clarence.

"Why in the world is this fortune locked up in here when it can be put to such good use in the company?"

"Good question," acknowledged Clarence. "In fact, that is *the* question."

"So, what is *the* answer?" probed the CEO.

"The answer is the combination," revealed the janitor. "Some folks don't have the combination. Others have it, but forget it when they get busy. And if you don't know how to get into the vault, you can't get the fortune out and spread it around."

Then, setting his hand on Bill's shoulder, Clarence continued, "Maybe *you* can make sure that this fortune is spread around."

"But isn't that what we were doing when we framed the value statements and put them in every office?" asked Bill.

"I don't think so," replied Clarence. "When you think about it, those frames are just like this vault. Even though you can see the fortune, it's still locked up. And you still need the combination. That's where your speech comes in."

"I don't get it," said the confused CEO. "You told me the combination will be in the speech I'll deliver tomorrow. But I still don't understand what that means. What *is* the combination? How do we get to that fortune?"

"By *walking the talk*," revealed Clarence. "We get to the gold by walking the talk."

"There you go again with that 'walk the talk' stuff," complained Bill. "What's the connection?"

"It's like this," explained Clarence. "There's a fortune here in this vault, right?"

"Right!" agreed Bill. "You can see that yourself."

"Well, if all we do is talk about it, or show it to people, what good does it do us?"

"Not much good at all," responded Bill. "You have to use resources for them to be valuable."

"I think that's the connection you're looking for," offered the janitor. "We have to *use* the fortune for it to do us any good."

"So when we *talk* about values," concluded Bill, "we're just sitting on a fortune. The more we practice them, the more gold we set free. That must be the message we came here for. And the combination that's supposedly in my speech must be about *practicing* values."

Clarence confirmed Bill's discovery with nothing more than a smile.

The two men stood there looking at each other—basking in the glow of the CEO's discovery—when Bill once again heard a series of repeating chimes.

"Looks like it's time we continued our walk," suggested Clarence, as he removed his pocket watch and checked the face. "There are other things we need to see."

"You mean there's more?" asked Bill.

"A lot more!" answered the janitor.

Bill followed Clarence out of the vault. When both men had exited, the huge door closed and locked itself.

"That door," observed the CEO, "just closed by itself!"

"Amazing, isn't it," said Clarence as he pulled a red bandanna from his rear pocket and quickly cleaned the vault door before leaving.

"Amazing," said the CEO, "is an understatement. By the way, how did you know what was in there?"

"I've been in there a couple of times," answered Clarence, now leading the way back to the elevator. "Even a fortune can collect dust if you let it."

Bill checked his own watch as he passed by the old guard and approached the elevator doors. What he saw stopped him dead in his tracks. "It's the same time it was when we first got into the elevator!" he exclaimed.

"Yes, it is," confirmed the janitor with an ever-present smile. "I did promise this wouldn't take long. And, when you make a promise, you have to deliver. Speaking of that, maybe we should see what's keeping the fortune locked up in that vault."

Bill continued staring at his watch as he followed Clarence into the elevator.

When you make a promise, you have to deliver.

"Mr. Elby," said Clarence softly.

"I'm sorry," said the CEO, coming out of a trance-like state. "What is it you were saying?"

"Why don't we find out what's keeping that fortune locked in the vault?" repeated Clarence. "It's OK. Go ahead and push the next button."

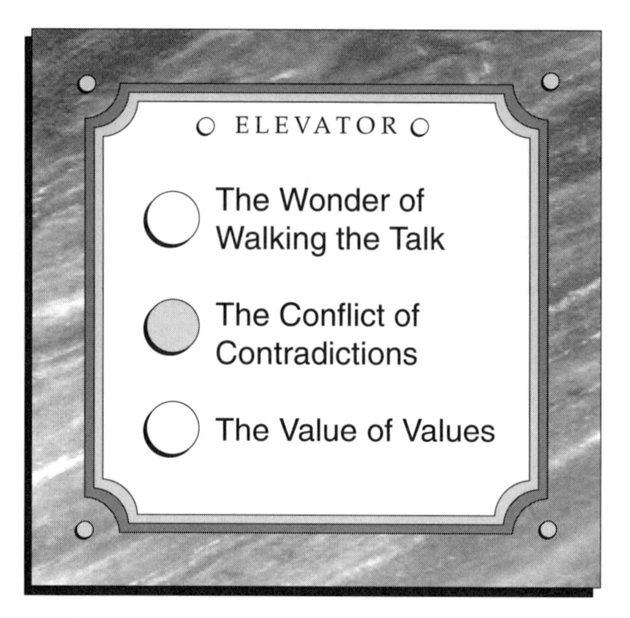

Still thinking about what had just occurred, Bill watched as his hand was drawn toward the control panel like steel to a magnet. He pushed the second button from the bottom, and the elevator doors closed.

The Conflict of Contradictions

This time, the doors immediately reopened into the longest and narrowest hallway that Bill had ever seen. Exiting the elevator was like stepping into a cold, dark tunnel. There was nothing but walls, floor, ceiling, and one barely visible door on the opposite end.

"Where are we now?" questioned Bill. "It's so dark here. Is this the basement?"

"Not exactly," responded the janitor. "But this is as low as we get."

Since he never cared for dark tunnels, Bill was careful to stay one step behind Clarence as they moved forward. After what seemed like an eternity of walking, they arrived at the door. A sign hanging over it identified and described the location of Bill's next learning experience: THE MUSEUM OF CORPORATE CONTRADICTIONS.

"This is where we'll see what's keeping the gold locked up in that vault," explained Clarence, as he turned the knob and pushed the door open.

Following the janitor through the doorway, Bill found himself in a room that was almost as big as the auditorium where he had been practicing his speech. The walls and floor were filled with display cases and museum exhibits. Each was individually illuminated by a spotlight.

"What are these things?"

"Well," answered Clarence, "the sign over the door says these are contradictions, but I call them 'unconscious do anothers.'"

"Unconscious do anothers?"

"You know. That's when we say one thing, but unconsciously *do another*. At least most of the time they're unconscious."

Rather than question Clarence any further about the museum contents, Bill decided to find out for himself. Taking the lead, he headed for the exhibits on his right and then stopped in front of the display closest to the museum entrance. This first item—which would offer only a small preview of things to come—immediately drew his attention. There, hanging on the wall, was an enlargement of a two-year-old newspaper article. The headline read: TREEVIEW MANAGERS TAKE BIG BONUSES IN LEAN TIMES. The article went on to describe how Bill's predecessor and senior staff were awarded large year-end bonuses for keeping the company alive during a financially troubled period.

"What do you see here?" asked Clarence.

Because he had always been sensitive to the subject of executive compensation, Bill immediately recognized the contradiction. "It seems my predecessors cut back on everything. Everything, that is, except their own compensation."

"It does seem that way," agreed the janitor.

"But they did save the company," rationalized the CEO. "We wouldn't be standing here now if they hadn't."

"Did they do it all by themselves?"

"Of course not. Everyone had to pitch in to make their plans work."

"But everyone didn't get the money," added Clarence. "And everyone knows it."

"I *got* the point!" exclaimed Bill.

"In this case, I think you *inherited* the point," sympathized Clarence.

"Are there many examples like this one in here?"

"Everything here represents a contradiction in some way or another," answered the janitor. "But most aren't as obvious as this one. That's why I call them *unconscious* do anothers. You really have to think about some of this stuff to figure it out. That next one is a good example."

Moving further into the room, Bill found a two-foot square glass case. Inside the case was a small pedestal that supported one single paper clip.

"Where's the display?" inquired the CEO. "There's nothing here but a paper clip."

"That's it!" replied Clarence. "The paper clip *is* the display."

"Now I see what you mean about things not being obvious. What's the significance of the clip? What does this have to do with contradictions?"

"I wondered the same thing the first time I saw this. Then, I found out that the clip has *everything* to do with contradictions. Do you know how many people have to approve buying one carton of those clips, and how long it takes to get them?"

"No, I don't know. I really don't spend much time getting involved with paper clips."

"Well, the answer is *two*," revealed the janitor. "It says it right there on the side of the case. Two people to approve them, and two weeks to get them. If it's two approvals and two weeks for paper clips, you can imagine what it must be for other things."

"But we do need to control expenses."

"I understand. But one of our values talks about making decisions at the lowest possible level. Maybe that's where the real cost control needs to be. Otherwise, you have . . ."

"A contradiction," interrupted Bill.

"A contradiction!" confirmed Clarence, as the two men left the glass case and continued their journey through the museum.

The next display item to capture Bill's focus was a red metal case labeled: SUPERVISOR'S TOOL BOX. "What's in there?" he asked.

"Let's find out," suggested Clarence. "Go ahead and open it up."

Bill unsnapped the latch and lifted the lid. "It's empty!" he exclaimed. "There's nothing in here."

"It's empty all right," confirmed the janitor. "What do you suppose that means?"

"I guess the message is that supervisors don't always have the tools they need to do their jobs."

"Seems like that could be a big problem," acknowledged Clarence. "If you want to get the job done, you've got to have the right tools. Either you've got 'em when they hire you, or the company's got to give them to you. But I've seen a lot of supervisors walking around here with empty tool boxes. They're doing the best they can, but they could do a lot better."

"Tell me Clarence, what kind of tools do *you* see some supervisors lacking?"

"People type tools, mostly. They've got to be able to talk to folks and treat them the way our values say. It's just like in sports—they need to be good coaches and help folks do their very best. And they need to know the right way to deal with people who don't work the way they should. I think they can get those tools in training programs."

"That's very interesting," responded Bill, "because I'm constantly getting complaints from managers who claim we're spending a fortune on training. They feel they're always in the classroom instead of on the job."

"Well," replied Clarence, "maybe they're getting the wrong kind of training. And maybe there's more to it than just training. All I know is if supervisors don't have the tools they need, we've got another contradiction."

"Because we're expecting them to do a job, but not preparing them to do it."

"Yes sir. And that doesn't make much sense. We wouldn't allow someone to operate a piece of equipment unless they knew how. But sometimes we let people supervise others when they don't know how. That's probably *not* the best way to deal with what those values call 'our most important resource.' What do you think?"

"I think I'm starting to understand the significance of this room," the CEO acknowledged softly. "I'd like to see more."

"I was hoping you'd say that," said Clarence, with a nod of approval. "I think you'll find the next one very interesting."

Continuing to their left, the two men stopped in front of a jamb which supported a half-open door. Mounted in the middle of the door was a brass plaque engraved: THE PROVERBIAL OPEN DOOR POLICY.

"Wait just a minute," said Bill, in an annoyed tone. "I have a real problem with this one. An open door policy is an invitation for employees to discuss their problems and concerns with management. It's a great idea based on good intentions. How can that possibly contradict our values?"

"It doesn't," answered Clarence.

"Then why is this here?" demanded Bill.

"I think my grandpa had the answer to that one," suggested the janitor. "He used to say 'we judge ourselves mostly by our intentions, but others judge us mostly by our actions.' You see, the idea or the intention of that open door isn't the problem. The problem is how that idea is used. It's what you find on the other side of the door that's the contradiction. Why don't we see what's there."

We judge ourselves mostly by our intentions, but others judge us mostly by our actions.

Bill stepped onto the platform and pushed the door completely open. What he saw astonished him. "There's nothing here!" he exclaimed. "No lights, no walls—no anything. This is a passage to nowhere!"

"You're right about that," confirmed Clarence. "There's *nothing* on the other side of that open door. Do you see the contradiction now?"

"This implies that our open door policy is nothing more than a nice gesture; that there's no real open communication and problem solving taking place. I can't believe that's true in every case!"

"Seems like it doesn't have to happen in every case for it still to be a contradiction. I'm afraid more than just a few employees see that open door just as it is here."

"That explains why so few people actually use it," Bill concluded.

"You mean it's not because folks just don't have any problems?" asked the janitor with a coy grin.

"No, Clarence. I'll bet you know better than that. I understand the contradiction here."

"Just checking." The old man's warm smile suggested that he was truly pleased with Bill's progress.

After stopping at a few more displays and seeing more contradictions, Bill's attention was drawn to the exhibit which took up most of the museum's back wall. There, he saw another glass case housing a variety of small items. On the wall, above the case, was a large electronic scoreboard—the kind you find on any game field. But instead of the usual HOME and VISITORS, it displayed "scores" under categories labeled US and THEM.

"Let me guess," proposed the CEO, "this exhibit depicts the 'us versus them' syndrome."

"I don't know about any syndromes, but there sure are some *do anothers* in here. Take a gander at the display case."

The first items Bill saw as he looked through the glass were two small metal signs. One read MANAGEMENT PARKING ONLY, the other EXECUTIVE DINING ROOM.

"What do you see there?" tested Clarence as he pointed to the signs.

"Obviously," answered Bill in a somewhat defensive tone, "these are perks. They're examples of the few privileges that come with the responsibility of position. In a small way, they make up for the long hours many of us put in—but don't get paid for." Then after a quick pause, Bill turned the table on the janitor. "What do *you* see?"

"Well, I see privileges all right, and I'm sure you deserve them. But I also see *contradictions*. It's not the parking spots or the dining room themselves—it's what they represent."

"What do you mean?"

"Let me put it this way," replied Clarence. "Do you remember the very last line in all those frames you've put up on the walls everywhere?"

"Yes, I do. Our values statements end with the words 'we're all in this together.'" The second he finished his answer, Bill smiled. Then, realizing he'd been had by the crafty old janitor, the CEO continued. "And you can't tell people that we're all in this together, but still have special benefits for a select few, right?"

"I couldn't have said it any better myself," complimented the janitor.

"Somehow I think he could," thought the CEO as he moved to his left to examine more of the *us versus them* exhibit. In the far end of the case, he found a copy of a written report to management which described grievance, arbitration and litigation activities for a past year. The information was broken down under two main categories: those "won" by the company and those "won" by employees.

"Don't bother asking me what I see, Clarence," instructed Bill. "The contradiction is as clear as it can be. Our talk says we're a team, but behaviors like this say we're really adversaries."

"I'm afraid so," agreed the janitor. "My old grandpa knew about this one too. He taught me that people hear what we say, but they see what we do. And seeing is believing."

"Your grandfather must have been a very wise man. His words certainly apply to me."

"How's that?"

"I'm seeing," answered Bill, "and I'm definitely starting to believe."

With that, Clarence motioned for Bill to lead the way to more do anothers.

People hear what we say, but they see what we do.

And seeing is believing.

Bill's discomfort was slowly growing as more displays brought more contradictions to light.

He saw a paper target with one bullet hole outside of the target rings. This "one shot that missed the mark" symbolized Treeview's top-down, once-a-year performance appraisal process. This was a process that focused on production results and goal attainment, but failed to provide meaningful, timely feedback on teamwork, quality, people skills and many of the significant issues mentioned in the company's values statements.

Another display presented a painfully obvious contradiction. It was a glass case containing a brass token engraved with the word: EMPOWERMENT. Alongside it was a list of hundreds of work-related decisions made during the last few years without employee input or involvement.

On and on it went: display after display, contradiction after contradiction. The examples of *not* walking the talk seemed endless.

Then Bill came across the one item that drew his most serious attention. He had learned that everything in the museum was at least figuratively real. He hoped, however, that this startling display was an exception. There, in the corner of the room, was a guillotine.

"My gosh!" exclaimed the CEO as he looked up at the tall wooden tower and elevated blade. "What in the world is this doing here?"

"Scary, isn't it," replied Clarence.

Upon closer scrutiny, the president noticed an inscription on the blade: PERFORMANCE MANAGEMENT.

"This suggests that our approach to managing performance equates to cutting people's heads off!"

"I'm afraid so," confirmed Clarence. "At least in some cases."

Bill was truly dismayed by the janitor's comment. "How can that be?" he thought. "That's totally the opposite of our values." He literally interrogated Clarence for more information about the janitor's perspective on this apparent unconscious do another. The answers he received were as disturbing as the sight of the guillotine itself.

"Here's the way I see it," Clarence began, "most everybody here does a good job. And when you do a good job, you get left alone."

"What's wrong with that?" asked Bill. "We shouldn't bother employees when they do what we expect."

"I'm not talking about bothering folks," responded Clarence. "I'm talking about bothering *with* folks. It seems to me that people ought to thank you when you do a good job. And they should help you do an even better job the next time. That's what I tried to do when I coached my boy's little league team. But that doesn't always happen here. Not bothering with folks is the same as ignoring them. And that's like cutting their heads off."

"But we do have formal recognition awards for special achievement," argued Bill.

"Yes sir, we do. But that's mostly for big stuff," countered Clarence. "I'm talking about the everyday good job kinds of things. I guess some folks don't think it's important. But I sure do."

After a brief pause for Bill to consider what had been said, Clarence continued. "Sometimes we don't bother with people that have problems until the problems get real big. Then guess what happens?"

"We're forced to issue discipline," answered the CEO.

"That's right! They get warned and reprimanded and eventually sent home without pay. It's just like when I was a kid and I acted up. I'd get reprimanded and sent to my room without supper. You see," concluded Clarence, "sometimes no matter what we do, we get our heads cut off. And what goes around *does* come around."

"So," replied Bill after a moment of reflection, "we unconsciously contradict our own values when we punish our most important and valuable resource."

Clarence merely nodded his head. No other response seemed necessary.

"What else do we need to see in here?" asked Bill.

"Only two more to go."

"Thank goodness! I don't think I could take much more of this," said the CEO as he followed Clarence to the next exhibit.

The two men stopped in front of the display labeled: THE POWER OF PERCEPTIONS. There, Bill saw a large photograph of the Treeview complex hanging over a small table. On the table sat several pairs of eyeglasses.

"Take a look at the picture," requested Clarence. "What do you see?"

"Our administration building and production facility," responded the CEO. "What am I supposed to see?"

Without answering, Clarence picked up a pair of glasses from the table and handed them to Bill. "Why don't you try it with these."

After slipping the glasses on, Bill saw a much different and somewhat shocking picture.

"Now what do you see?" inquired Clarence.

"I see barbed wire, window bars, and towers. This is a picture of a prison!"

Bill quickly removed the glasses and began inspecting the frames. He found an inscription which read: EMPLOYEE PERSPECTIVE.

Before the CEO could say a word, Clarence handed him another pair. "Try these," the janitor suggested. "The frames are marked 'customer perspective.'"

"Now I see a fortress," revealed the CEO after switching glasses. "It's a castle surrounded by a big moat filled with alligators. And, the drawbridge is up. There's no way to get to it."

"Seems like our company looks different to different folks. There's more glasses here, and each of them will show you a different picture."

"Do all employees and customers see the company this way?"

"Some do," answered Clarence. "And others see it completely different."

"So how do we know what they all see?"

"Most of the time we don't know. I think that's because we just don't ask. Sometimes we ask, but then don't do anything with what people tell us. Both of those kinda send a message that we don't care."

"Another contradiction," Bill concluded.

"A big fat one," confirmed Clarence.

Following Clarence to the final exhibit area, Bill grew increasingly somber from the weight of all the contradictions he had seen.

"I'll need some help with this last one," suggested the janitor as the two men passed into an alcove identified with three-dimensional brass letters: THE HALLOWED HALLS OF HALF-HEARTED PROGRAMS.

Upon entering the alcove, Bill's attention was immediately drawn to a sign on the wall: PROGRAMS OF THE YEAR. Underneath the sign was a series of company-sponsored initiatives—listed according to the year they had been implemented. The list read like a "what's what" of once popular human resources endeavors. Last year's program was a safety improvement effort called *Safety Now*. The year before brought *Circles of Quality*. And before that it was *Managing By Objectives*.

"Seems like everything in here was a good idea that just never worked out," offered Clarence. "Whenever I hear people talk about these things, they always start with the words: 'whatever happened to.' Why do you suppose that is?"

Switching roles from student to teacher, Bill called upon his experience as a manager to answer the janitor's question. "Programs usually fail for one of two reasons," he explained. "Either they're bad ideas to begin with, or they're good ideas that are handled poorly. Since these are all basically good ideas, the problem must have been in how they were implemented."

"Then that must be where the contradictions are," Clarence concluded.

"Probably so. Most of the programs on that list happened before I got here. I'd guess they were developed by staff groups and then peddled to senior management without the input of the people who have to make them work. If that was the case, they were doomed to failure before they began. And that's too bad because I'll bet we pumped a fortune into them."

"Boy, that's for sure," confirmed Clarence. "I remember all kinds of bells and whistles when each of these first came out. Maybe they put the wrong kind of fortune into them. Maybe they needed the kind of fortune that's in the vault."

"That's a fact!" came a voice from the corner of the room. Looking toward the sound, Bill saw a portly woman in her sixties wearing a green eye shade. "I'm Catherine," she said. "I'm the curator of corporate contradictions. I run this place, and I can tell you that everything you said is true."

"Hello, Catherine," said the CEO as he extended his hand. "I'm Bill Elby. I guess I run this place also."

"I know who you are," replied the gruff yet likable character. "Is Clarence giving you an eyeful?"

"An eyeful *and* an earful."

"Good. I'd show you around myself, but I'm getting ready for a new program of the year. It's a doosie and it should be coming any day now. I'm going to put it right there in the corner."

"What program is that?" inquired the CEO.

"It's called TQP . . . that stands for *Treeview Quality Process*."

"What!" exclaimed Bill. "Wait a second. The quality process was my idea. That's my baby!"

"Ooops!" exclaimed Catherine. "Sorry to be the one to break the news to you, but *your baby* does seem to meet our criteria for program of the year. If things don't change, it will be in here real soon." Then, sensing that Bill was on the verge of shooting the messenger, Catherine politely excused herself and quickly returned to work.

"How could this be?" thought Bill to himself. Although it was hard for him to accept what Catherine had said, deep inside he knew there was little reason to doubt the validity of her message.

"I guess that last one really hit home," observed Clarence.

"More than you could ever imagine."

"Well, at least we're through," consoled Clarence. "Has this helped explain why that fortune stays locked up in the vault?"

"All too well," answered Bill as he stared at the ground. "The fortune stays locked up when our behavior contradicts our values, when we don't walk the talk—like all these examples."

"Absolutely!" exclaimed Clarence, trying to cheer up the CEO. "I'm proud of you."

"Thanks, but this has been a very depressing experience. I knew some of these things existed, but I never saw them as contradictions until now. There's no way in the world I can talk about values in that speech tomorrow after seeing this."

"Don't worry," said the optimistic janitor. "We're not finished yet. We've only seen the bad news. There's also good news . . ."

Clarence was interrupted by the now familiar sound of repeating chimes. Then, tapping his right pants pocket, he continued. "We need to see that good news. It's time we took a walk."

The janitor took the lead as the two men headed for the museum doorway.

As he walked, Bill wrestled with what he had just seen. "What am I going to say tomorrow?" he wondered. "How can I possibly give people the combination to the vault, and show them how to get to the gold, when I'm not sure how to do it myself?" He was so engrossed in thought that he failed to notice that the museum door opened directly into the elevator. The long, dark hallway had disappeared.

"Now it's time to push that top button," said the janitor, pointing to the elevator control panel.

"What was that?" asked Bill after a few more seconds of deep thought.

"Why don't you push that top button—the one you wanted to push when we first started."

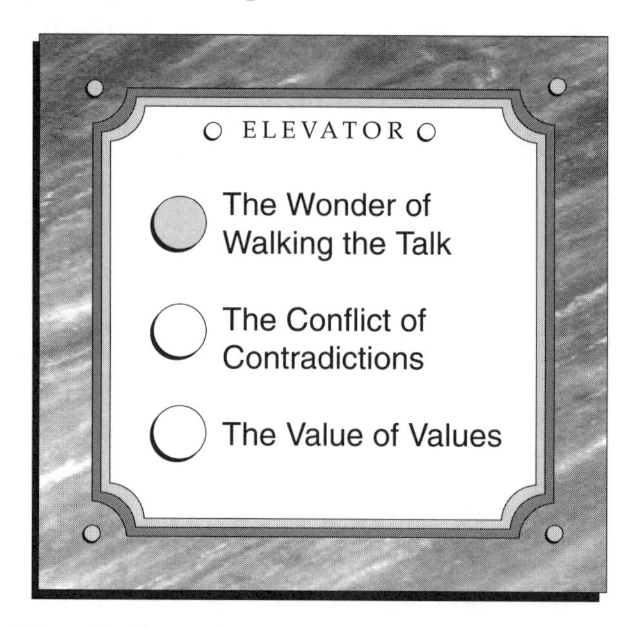

"Finally!" exclaimed Bill. "I hope the news here is as good as you say it is. I could use some right about now." With that, he pushed the button labeled: The Wonder of Walking The Talk. And, as he had come to expect, the elevator doors closed.

The Wonder of Walking The Talk

Bill sensed his next experience would be much more positive the moment the elevator doors reopened.

There, on the other side, was a large room filled with very productive people doing very different jobs. Some stood at machines while others sat at desks. Some worked with customers; others worked with tools. But they all had one thing in common: everyone seemed as bright and cheerful as the room itself.

Clearly, something special was happening here, and the CEO could hardly wait to find out what it was.

As he exited the elevator, Bill noticed a rather dramatic change in his wardrobe. Looking down, he found he was wearing a janitor's uniform just like Clarence's. "Wait a second," he said, grabbing the janitor by the arm. "What happened to my clothes?"

"I forgot to tell you about that," answered Clarence. "I think you'll find it easier to see things when you're one of us. This way, nobody will recognize you. And besides, people don't pay much attention to janitors."

"But how did I get these . . ."

"Don't worry about the clothes," interrupted the janitor. "You'll get your tie back soon enough. Just enjoy the freedom and look around for now. There's a lot to see." Then Clarence grinned and added, "By the way, you look pretty good in khakis."

"Gee, thanks," said the CEO sarcastically. "I guess this is no stranger than anything else that's happened today."

With that, Bill refocused his attention on the room. What he observed literally took his breath away. Everywhere he looked, he saw GOLD. Bricks of gold, like he had seen in the vault, were stacked on desks, on shelves, on machines, and on the floor. And the light reflecting from all those bricks bathed everything and everyone in a warm, golden hue.

"Where are we?" asked Bill. "What is this place, and who are these people?"

"The folks that work here call this the 'Success Department,'" answered Clarence. "Everyone here has the combination. They all walk the talk."

"Everyone?" inquired the CEO.

"Yes sir, everyone!" confirmed the janitor. "Bosses and workers. And that's what makes them so successful."

"Just how successful are they?"

"See for yourself," suggested Clarence as he pointed to a series of productivity graphs on the wall.

"They're off the top of the charts," said Bill in amazement. "If those figures are accurate, these have to be the most productive people I've ever seen."

"Me too," added the janitor. "Those figures are accurate all right. These people *are* productive . . . and they're just as enthusiastic as they are productive."

"This is all the result of walking the talk?" probed Bill.

"It sure is!"

"Then I guess I don't totally understand. How does practicing our values lead to productivity? And enthusiasm?"

"It's really pretty simple when you think about it," suggested Clarence. "Good things happen when you make sure that good things happen!"

Bill paused and then responded in an exasperated tone, "The last thing I need right now is a bunch of double-talk!"

"It's not double-talk at all," assured the janitor. "The way I see it, those values we put in frames are good things. Right?"

"Of course they are," confirmed Bill.

"Well then, if we make sure that people really do them, why shouldn't we expect good things to happen?"

Good things happen when you make sure that good things HAPPEN!

"The other side of that is just as true," continued Clarence. "If people don't do things according to those good values, why *should* we expect good things to happen?"

"No reason," replied Bill. "In either case."

"Exactly!"

"This is all starting to come together," acknowledged the CEO. "Our values are good things—our corporate gold. But they stay locked up in the vault until we actually practice them. And, many times we unconsciously do things that prevent us from getting the gold out. That's what I saw in the museum."

"Right!"

"But when we do practice those values, good things happen."

"Amen to common sense," chuckled Clarence.

"So how is it that all these people have the combination?" pursued Bill. "Where did they get it?"

"Mostly they got it from three people," answered Clarence. "Karen, Willie, and Mike."

"Who are they?"

"Karen Cooke is the manager here. Everyone calls her 'By-the-Book' Karen Cooke. Then there's the supervisor, 'Say-Do' Willie LaRue. And 'Golden Rule' Mike O'Toole is one terrific worker. Karen, Willie, and Mike are pretty much responsible for sharing the combination with everyone else who works here."

"I suppose there's some significance to those nicknames."

"There sure is," confirmed Clarence. "Those aren't just nicknames. They're also clues."

"Clues to the combination?" asked the CEO.

"Yes," said the janitor, "clues to the combination. There's a lot we can learn about walking the talk from these pros. What do you say we start with Karen Cooke."

"By-the-Book" Karen Cooke

Clarence took the CEO to an open door at the back of the room. "This is Karen's office," he said, pointing to an unoccupied desk.

"Where is she?" asked Bill.

"Probably out on the floor somewhere working with folks. That's where she usually is."

"So what is it that's so special about Karen?" inquired Bill. "How long has she been here, and what's her background?"

"I think we'll find everything we need to know about her right inside here."

As they entered the office, Bill noticed a nameplate on the front of the desk. It read: BY-THE-BOOK KAREN COOKE.

"Why do they call her that?" he asked.

"Because that's how she does everything—by the book."

"That's not exactly the most flattering nickname to have," suggested Bill. "That label usually implies inflexibility."

"Well, she is pretty inflexible when it comes to the book. But whether the label is flattering or not kinda depends on which *book* you're talking about. Don't you think?"

"So which book are we talking about?"

"That one right there," answered Clarence as he pointed to the framed Treeview value statements hanging on Karen's office wall. "*That's* the book she goes by."

Then, pointing to another frame on the wall, Clarence continued. "And there's her personal combination."

Gazing at that second frame, Bill read Karen Cooke's five simple rules for walking the talk.

WALKING THE TALK
(By-the-Book Behavior)

1. START WITH ME
2. FIND OTHERS WHO BELIEVE
3. SHOW THEM HOW
4. HOLD THEM ACCOUNTABLE
5. DO RIGHT BY THOSE WHO DO RIGHT

"So these are Karen's secrets to getting to all that gold?" inquired Bill.

"Yes sir," replied the janitor. "But they're not really secrets. She shares them with everyone. More importantly, she follows those rules all the time."

"How do you know?"

"I've heard people talking, and I've seen it for myself."

"Since you seem to know so much about this, maybe you can explain her rules to me," requested Bill.

"I'll try," responded Clarence. "Let's take that first rule: *start with me*. When it comes to walking the talk, she always starts with herself. She sets the example. Karen never expects people to act a certain way unless she does it first. I found out that her favorite words are 'check it.' She checks everything she does, and every rule she makes, against the Treeview values *before* she does them. If they don't fit, she looks for different ways that do fit. Simple isn't it?"

"This is very interesting," said the CEO. "Keep going."

"OK. Look at rule two: *find others who believe*. When she needs to hire people, Karen tries hard to find folks who feel that the company values are really important. You see, Karen understands that values are the key to success, and she wants the people who work for her to be successful. One thing's for sure, if you want to get promoted here, you've got to believe and behave by the book!"

"So value-alignment is one of her selection and promotion criteria," summarized the CEO.

"Yes indeed," said Clarence with a laugh, "except I would have said it in English."

"Sorry about that! Please continue. Tell me about rule three . . . in English."

"Karen's third rule is *show them how*. She's not only a good boss, she's a good teacher, too. She spends a lot of time showing people how to work by the book. And each time she does, she gives them a little gold. Karen makes sure that all the training programs her folks go to teach things that match the company values, and she talks about it with them when they get back so they understand the connection. And she's helped the supervisors develop their own rules for walking the talk."

"She's obviously a very effective manager," acknowledged Bill.

"All the folks who work here would definitely agree with that. Now," continued the janitor, "where was I? Oh yeah, rule four. Rule four is *hold them accountable*, and this is where you see what a real stickler Karen is. With her, it's not enough to just get results. You also have to get those results according to the values . . . according to the book."

"So the *means* to the ends are just as important as the ends themselves," clarified Bill.

"You bet!" confirmed the janitor. "In fact, Karen says, 'the better the means, the better the ends.' When it comes time for evaluations or promotions, she looks at what you did *and* how you did it. And she's always letting people know what she expects and where they stand. It's kinda funny."

"What's funny?"

"Karen found out the people here all expect the same thing she does: whatever you do, do it by the book."

"Let me take a crack at the last rule," offered Bill. "*Do right by those who do right.* I suspect that Karen takes care of people who meet her expectations. She believes that good things should happen to people who do good things. And she probably makes sure they do happen!"

"Well done!" exclaimed Clarence. "By the way, guess what else Karen found out?"

"What's that?"

"The more good things she does for people, the more good things they do in return."

"I guess it's true that reinforced behavior is repeated behavior," concluded the CEO.

"I guess so," agreed the janitor. "And it all happens by the book."

"So this is why Karen is so successful. I sure would like to meet her."

"In a sense, you already have. You know what's important to her. And when you know that, you know her. Besides, she's probably busy right now. I'm sure she's out there somewhere walking the talk."

Then pointing to a man walking toward them, Clarence continued. "But *there's* someone who works for Karen that you *can* meet. That's 'Say-Do' Willie LaRue. He's the supervisor here. Come on, I'll introduce you."

"Say-Do" Willie LaRue

"Hey, Willie," said Clarence, greeting the approaching supervisor. "What's goin' on?"

"Lotsa stuff, Clarence," said Willie returning the greeting as he shook the janitor's hand. "How are you?"

"Just fine, thanks."

"Great."

"Willie, there's someone here I'd like you to meet. This is Bill. He's new here."

"Hey, Bill!" exclaimed the supervisor. "Welcome to the team. What position do you play?"

Sensing that Bill wasn't sure how to respond, Clarence answered for him. "Clean-up. Bill plays clean-up."

"Well, we can always use good folks in the clean-up spot. Glad you're here."

"Thanks very much," responded the unrecognized CEO. "It's good to be here."

"Sorry I can't stay and talk," apologized Willie, "but I told a few of my folks that we'd get together. Their time is important. And besides, when you say something, you gotta do it! You have to follow the game plan."

"I understand," replied Bill. "Nice to meet you, Willie."

"You too, Bill!"

"Willie seems like a great guy," said Bill.

"He's the best," confirmed Clarence. "He used to play semi-pro baseball. That's how he got his nickname. You've heard the story about Babe Ruth pointing into the stands and then hitting a home run where he pointed?"

"Sure I have."

"Well Willie used to do that all the time. He'd say what he was going to do, and then he'd do it."

"So how come he stopped playing ball?" asked the CEO.

"Because he just couldn't deliver anymore. Willie's got a basic rule: *If you can't do it, don't say it. And if you can't say it, don't play it.* That's why he stopped playing baseball and moved on to being a supervisor here. He found out he likes coaching even more than he liked playing. And boy is he a good coach."

"Because he always does what he says he's going to do?"

"Absolutely!" answered Clarence. "And because he always follows the game plan."

If you can't do it,
don't say it.
And if you can't say it,
don't play it.

"What do you mean by game plan?" asked Bill.

"When Willie played ball, they always had a game plan. They'd figure out what each player needed to do and how they all needed to work together in order to win. Once they thought it through and were sure it was a good plan, the only thing left to do was to *do it*. The more they followed the plan, the more they won. That's why they kept doing it."

"Well, what exactly is Willie's game plan?" questioned the CEO. "As a supervisor, I mean."

"He keeps it over there on his desk," said Clarence. "Let's go take a look."

Clarence took Bill to a desk in the middle of the room and picked up a brown folder labeled: GAME PLAN.

"Here," said Clarence as he handed the folder to Bill. "See for yourself."

Bill opened the folder and found that Willie LaRue had his own personal combination to the vault.

THE GAME PLAN

(Say-Do Behavior)

1. PLAY BY THE RULES

2. DON'T WAIT FOR SOMEONE ELSE TO MAKE ALL THE CALLS

3. GO FOR SINGLES RATHER THAN HOME RUNS

4. TREAT EVERYONE LIKE A TOP DRAFT CHOICE

5. LET EVERYONE HOLD THE TROPHY

"What do you know about Willie's game plan?" asked Bill.

"I know he always follows it," answered Clarence. "And, I know it works. I can tell just by looking around."

"What does he mean by *play by the rules*? What do rules have to do with values?"

"Willie thinks of the values as part of the company rules. He says we wouldn't have them and talk about them if we didn't expect people to *follow* them. His view on rules is pretty simple: we're either following them or we're breaking them. There's not much in between."

"I've just recently come to realize how true that is," confessed Bill.

"Willie says that playing by the rules means pointing out when someone isn't following them," continued the janitor. "He lets Karen know when her plans don't match the values, and he expects all of his people to do the same with him."

"So Willie feels that *everyone* is responsible for walking the talk," concluded the CEO.

"You bet. But when it comes to responsibility, Willie always looks in the mirror first. That explains his second game plan rule: *don't wait for someone else to make all the calls*. You see, Willie developed this game plan himself. He didn't wait for Karen to give it to him. He ran it by her to make sure he was on track, but the point is he didn't wait. Willie says part of a supervisor's job is figuring things out. And, if Willie says it, you can bet your last dollar that Willie does it!"

"How about this third rule," pursued the CEO, "*go for singles rather than home runs*?"

"Willie explained that one to me a long time ago," said Clarence. "When he played ball, he learned that you win more games with a lot of singles than you do with a few home runs. He discovered the same was true when he became a supervisor. For Willie, walking the talk means doing a bunch of little things according to the values every day, rather than one big thing every once in a while."

"So little things *do* mean a lot."

"No question about it. Besides, we can't do really big things every day. If we're really serious about walking the talk all the time, we have to focus on the small stuff."

"What kind of small stuff are you talking about?"

"The way we talk to people. How we hold meetings and listen to what others have to say. The way we deal with folks when their work is good *and* when it's not. And the kind of examples we set. Those are the little things that Willie pays attention to."

"That explains his fourth game plan rule," concluded the CEO, "*treat everyone like a top draft choice*."

"Very good," acknowledged the janitor. "One of those value statements on the wall says, 'employees are our most important resource.' Willie not only believes that, he *behaves* it! He treats everybody like they have the stuff to be superstars. And he sees his job as helping them get there. That's what his baseball coach did for him. I think Willie's way of thanking his coach is to pass it on to others and teach them how to do the same."

"How about this last rule? I don't understand what he means by *let everyone hold the trophy.*"

"Talk to Willie, and he'll tell you that winning is a team sport. Nobody can do it alone. Heck, even athletes in one-person sports have coaches, and trainers, and other folks that help them. Teamwork is *everything* to Willie. He's got this great attitude: his people don't work for him, he works for them. His number one job is to help people be successful. He wins when the team wins. And when that happens, he makes sure that everyone shares in the glory. Everyone gets to hold the trophy!"

"That's very admirable," offered the CEO.

"Everybody here admires him," shared Clarence. "Especially the folks he supervises. And it's easy to see why they do."

Then handing Bill a business card, Clarence continued, "Here's someone else everyone admires." The card read:

Golden Rule Mike O'Toole
In Sync Team Member

"Golden Rule" Mike O'Toole

"I think I've got this one figured out," stated Bill. "Mike treats people the way he wants to be treated. Right?"

"That's right. Mike's been here about two years now, and he definitely follows the 'golden rule.'"

"That's a great quality. If more people followed that simple guide, the world would be a much better place to live in."

"For sure," agreed the janitor.

Bill examined the card and then continued, "What's this under his name: 'in sync team member'?"

"That's Mike's title. Willie gave it to him."

"What does it mean?" probed Bill.

"It means that he walks the talk," explained Clarence. "He tries very hard to make sure whatever he does is in sync with the company values."

"Well this is one employee I've *got* to meet!"

"I wish you could," responded the janitor, "but he's not here today. He's in training."

"What program is he attending?" asked Bill.

"Oh, he's not attending. He's teaching!"

"That's an interesting switch. What is he teaching?"

"His combination," answered Clarence. "He's showing some of the other folks how *he* gets to the gold."

"And what might that combination be?"

"It's right there on the back of his card. Flip it over."

Following Clarence's instructions, Bill turned the card over and found Mike O'Toole's combination.

1. Give whatever you expect
2. Have great expectations

"Mike says that you earn the right to expect others to do things by doing those things yourself," continued the janitor. "If we expect management to follow the values, we have to follow them ourselves. Otherwise, we'd be hypocrites. And Mike *hates* hypocrites with a passion."

"Most people do," added Bill. "But tell me, Clarence, what specifically does Mike do to walk the talk? Does he have a list of rules like Karen? Or a game plan like Willie?"

"Nothing that detailed. Mostly, he just has great expectations."

"Great expectations?"

"Yes. He knows that the more he expects, the more he has to give. When he's dealing with customers, or fellow workers, or even the bosses, he thinks about how he would want to be dealt with. Then he does that himself. He makes sure he walks the talk by expecting others to do the same."

"That almost seems too simplistic," countered Bill. "Does that work in the real world?"

"I hear that term 'real world' a lot. It seems to me the real world isn't a place as much as it is a bunch of actions—it's whatever we do. If people say something doesn't work in the real world, maybe it's because they just aren't doing it. If I choose to do something different, and I do it enough, eventually it will become the real world. At least, that's what I think."

"You know, I believe you're right," said the CEO after pondering Clarence's words. "And that's been the point you've been making in all the places you've taken me. Our values only become our real world when we walk the talk. When we fail to do that, people are left hearing one thing but seeing something quite different. What they *see* is their real world, and they respond accordingly."

"You know what?" asked Clarence.

"What's that?"

"I think you're ready to give that speech."

"Maybe. But I wouldn't mind staying a little longer and watching these people mine more gold."

"Don't worry. I have a feeling you'll be seeing these folks again. Besides," continued Clarence as he pulled the chiming watch from his pocket, "it's time we moved on."

Upon returning to the elevator, Bill realized that there were no other buttons to push on the control panel.

"How do we get out of here?" he asked. "I've already used all the buttons here."

"Why don't you push the top one again," suggested Clarence.

Completely trusting the old janitor's instruction, the CEO pushed the last button with no hesitation.

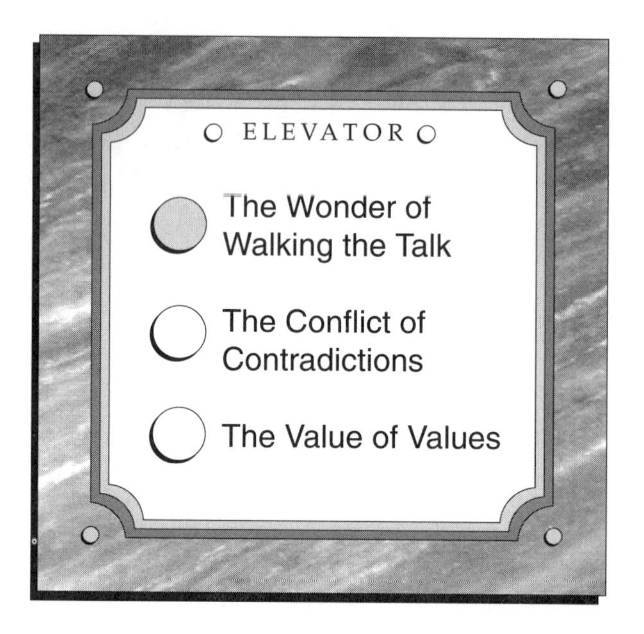

As the elevator doors closed, Bill stretched to get one final look at this very special place.

The Vision

As the elevator doors reopened, Bill could see that he had returned to the empty company auditorium where he had been practicing his speech. He greeted the familiar surroundings with a sigh of both relief and disappointment. He was happy to finally come to a place he recognized, but also saddened by the realization that his strange yet memorable journey was apparently coming to an end.

"Clarence," said the CEO as he stepped out of the elevator wearing his original suit and tie, "this has been one of the strangest experiences of my life."

No response followed Bill's remark.

After a moment of silence, Bill turned around and discovered why the janitor had not replied. No one was there. Clarence had disappeared along with the elevator doors.

"What in the world!" Bill exclaimed, as he ran his fingers across the auditorium wall desperately searching for the elevator that wasn't there.

"Clarence! Where are you?" he shouted as he looked around the empty room. Again there was no response. "C'mon, Clarence, you were here just a second ago. You *were* here . . . weren't you?"

The only sound Bill heard was the faint echo of his own words. Then, trying to regain his bearings, he looked at his watch. Exactly sixty seconds had passed from the time he first entered the elevator—if he ever entered an elevator at all.

"Could I have imagined all of this?" wondered the CEO who was now starting to doubt not only the entire experience, but also his own sanity. "What really took place during that lost minute?"

Finding no answers in the room, Bill returned to the podium, picked up his speech notes, and headed for his office.

"How did the rehearsal go?" asked Bill's administrative assistant as the CEO passed her desk.

"It was . . ."

"It was what?" she asked.

"It was strange, Maria," he said with a blank stare. "Very strange."

Bill walked past the assistant who immediately stood up and followed him into his office.

"Are you all right?" she asked.

"Oh, I'm fine, Maria," he replied. "Thanks for asking. I just have a lot to think about right now."

As Maria left, Bill plopped himself in his desk chair and began rummaging through his speech notes. After a few seconds of paper sorting, he put the notes down, sat back in his chair, and began to recall what had happened in the auditorium. Closing his eyes, Bill clearly saw Clarence's image and heard the first of the janitor's many profound lessons:

"Words to live by are just words,
unless you live by them."

Bill replayed that scene over and over again in his mind. When he finally opened his eyes, he was looking directly at the frame on his office wall that encased the Treeview value statements. Rising from his chair, he slowly walked across the room, removed the frame from the wall, and carried it back to his desk.

Bill methodically read through each of Treeview's values. While reading, he noticed that the reflection from his brass desk lamp gave the frame and its contents a bright yellow tint. He immediately thought of the vault and remembered the words he himself had spoken:

"Values are the gold that's in each of us . . . they're the real fortune of our organization."

"The combination," thought Bill, as he put the frame down. "I've got to give people the combination!" Then, closing his eyes one more time, he tried to recall the last stop on his journey: that enthusiastic and productive place where everyone had the combination, where everyone walked the talk. But the image that he saw was not as he remembered it. The faces and places were different. They were real! He saw people he recognized in actual Treeview locations doing actual Treeview work with real Treeview customers. Everyone was involved and tackled problems together. Trust and mutual respect were apparent everywhere. Good decisions were being made by people who actually did the work. And everyone had a stake in the company's success.

This was Bill's vision for Treeview. It was a place filled with people like Karen Cooke, Willie LaRue, and Mike O'Toole who made walking the talk priority one. It was a new corporate culture based on the timeless principle of reciprocity: what goes around, comes around.

What Bill saw was not utopia. There were imperfections. It was, however, a company of people with a tireless dedication to those few simple guidelines that appeared in wooden frames. It *was* achievable, and he knew it was his job, along with Treeview's managers and supervisors, to lead the way. "That is, after all, what leaders do," he thought.

Then, the CEO had the best vision of all. It was his second state of the company address to employees, one year later. He saw himself reporting dramatic increases in Treeview's productivity and profitability—all the result of a total company effort to walk the talk. Employees applauded each other in acknowledgment of such a successful turn-around. This was truly a picture worth savoring.

Suddenly, the CEO's thoughts were broken by the ringing of his phone. It was the facilities manager calling to confirm the arrangements for the next day's speech.

"We seem to be all set for tomorrow," said the voice on the other end of the line. "Just thought I'd check one last time to see if you needed anything."

Bill was about to respond, when he noticed a man pushing a janitor's cart past the open outer-office door. "Hold on," he said, practically dropping the phone as he made a beeline for the hallway. "Clarence?" he shouted. "Clarence, is that you?"

Stopping outside the door, Bill found the hallway unoccupied. There was neither a janitor nor a cart. It was just an empty corridor.

"I'd swear I saw Clarence," thought the CEO as he returned to his desk and the waiting phone call.

"Sorry about that," Bill told the manager. "I thought I saw someone I knew. Where were we?"

"No problem," replied the voice on the other end of the line. "I was just checking to see if you need anything for tomorrow."

"Actually, I could use a little more time. I've got several loose ends left to tie up."

"Anything I can do to help?" asked the manager.

"Not really," answered the CEO. "But thanks anyway. I'll be ready by tomorrow one way or another."

"Great! Listen, Bill," continued the manager, "you've got a lot of folks talking about your speech tomorrow. I'm really looking forward to getting some direction and hearing what you have to say. I guess, with the way the economy's been going and all the things happening in the world right now, you can certainly understand how people might be a little concerned about where we're going and how they all fit in."

"Seems reasonable," replied Bill. "I'm looking forward to hearing the speech myself."

Both men laughed. But Bill's laughter was tempered with concern. He knew the speech he had originally prepared somehow didn't seem right in light of the incredible journey he so vividly recalled.

"Well then, good luck tomorrow," said the manager. "I'll be looking forward to it."

Bill thanked the caller and hung up the phone. Leaning back in his chair, he once again began to wrestle over the images that seemed to relentlessly bombard his consciousness. He saw the little old janitor and heard his chiming watch. There was the elevator and the vault with those bars of gold inscribed with Treeview's corporate values.

Images and words were now coming faster than his ability to grasp them—the museum, the guillotine, contradictions, Karen Cooke, words to live by, the old guard, and the combination. On and on it continued until the pendulum clock on his wall began to chime. Suddenly, as if by some stroke of fate, it finally came to him. He understood what Clarence meant when he said the combination would be in his speech. After a few more moments of heavy thought, he tore his speech notes in half and threw them in his waste can.

Then, grabbing a pencil and blank pad, he began to write.

The Speech

The next morning, Bill arrived at the auditorium fifteen minutes before the scheduled start of his speech. He watched from the stage wings while the room quickly filled with employees. As the audience filed in and took their seats, Bill's anxiety level peaked. He wondered how the crowd would receive the message he had spent all night preparing. He wondered, and worried, and paced.

Finally, after what had to be the longest quarter-hour of his life, the waiting was over. It was time.

A hush fell over the room as he walked to the podium, positioned his handwritten notes, and began to speak.

fellow Treeview employees.
Good morning ~~ladies and gentlemen.~~
Before I begin my remarks, I'd like to tell you about a funny thing that happened to me on the way to the podium . . .

Bill's words were immediately met with polite laughter from several members of the audience who thought he was opening the speech with a traditional joke. As the laughter died, he continued.

. . . a funny thing really did happen to me on the way to the podium . . . I changed my presentation. Over the last few weeks, I've been struggling over exactly what I would say to all of you today. I wanted it to be meaningful, and I wanted it to be profound. In fact, I had prepared a specific speech which I rehearsed several times, but it just wasn't working . . . it just didn't feel right.

Then, yesterday, while I was here in this auditorium practicing my original speech for the last time, ~~someone~~ something came to me. I'm not sure whether you'd call it insight, or a vision, or just some new found common sense. But it was significant enough to cause me to tear up the old speech and work late last night trying to find the right words to share my thoughts and perspectives with you.

So, if you'll bear with me and this unrehearsed presentation, I'd like to talk about my view of this organization, a little about yesterday, and a lot about tomorrow.

After a short pause, Bill methodically worked his way through a series of visuals depicting the organization's financial picture, and then continued.

There are those who, considering the current economic realities, would suggest that Treeview is performing relatively well. And perhaps they're right. But debating that point would be counterproductive because that's not the real issue. The fact that global competition and economic challenges are here to stay means that even if today's performance is acceptable, it's not good enough to sustain us in the future. The two most important questions we must answer together are: what are we going to do about tomorrow, and how do we begin preparing for that reality today? That's what I'll spend the remainder of my time addressing. My guess is that's what you came to hear anyway.

Bill quickly checked his notes. The words "Vision—The Success Department" triggered a mental picture of that special place he had experienced—or perhaps only imagined—on the last stop of his journey with Clarence. With his memory full of yellow-gold images, happy faces, and positive productivity graphs, he pressed forward.

Many of you have been here a lot longer than I have. But regardless of our individual situations, I suspect that we share many beliefs and have a similar vision for this company. Looking to the future, I see . . .

As he spoke, Bill slowly scanned the sea of familiar faces. Certain ones reminded him of experiences they had weathered together. With a new sincerity in his tone, the CEO went on to describe his vision: a high quality and productive corporation, successfully meeting the challenges of the future through the talents existing within each employee.

Bill talked about trust, credibility, collaboration, consistency, and a host of similar attributes which shape the best of all working environments.

And then, he talked about prosperity . . . he talked about GOLD!

During the last year, I've spent a great deal of time in discussions and meetings trying to determine the best way to secure Treeview's future. I recall, at one of those meetings, someone humorously suggesting that what we needed was to discover a hidden fortune. My friends . . . yesterday I discovered such a fortune. It's one that's not really hidden, but it is sometimes hard to see.

A new stillness had quieted the room, and all eyes were riveted on the CEO. Bill noticed with a chuckle that Clark Spivey from purchasing had even turned up his hearing aid.

Feeling the affirmation of the crowd, Bill reached for a shelf inside the podium, grabbed a framed copy of the Treeview value statements and held it up for all to see.

Here is that fortune! For those of you who can't see what I'm holding, these are our Treeview company values. These are the real gold of our organization because they describe who we are and what, I think, we all envision for Treeview. This fortune has been here all along, and I've never fully recognized it. For that matter, maybe none of us have.

In the past, we've done a much better job of talking about these philosophies and values than living them. Well, that needs to change—for me and for all of us. Together we've got to make 'walking the talk' our top business priority. It's the only way we can meet the challenges of the future, and we need to start RIGHT NOW!

To get things going and to get everyone involved in walking the talk, we must start with a critical look at our Treeview values. Therefore, tomorrow I will ask that a task force be formed to examine each of our value statements. I would like this team to come out with recommendations as to how each statement might be improved and better used as a blueprint to run this company. Bottom line, folks: if these values are important enough to publish, they're important enough to live by.

The auditorium stirred with excitement as the CEO explained that *every* employee would be eligible to volunteer for the task force and that the selected team would represent all levels, departments, and points of view.

Although Bill felt the existing values were appropriate as written, he wanted to be sure. More importantly, he knew that creating the opportunity for involvement at all levels was the very best way to ensure both support and ownership of the values by the entire organization. It was participative; it was in sync; it was, in fact, "walking the talk."

Then, Bill recalled the *Museum of Corporate Contradictions* and began a new portion of the speech. He remembered the depression he experienced upon discovering the existence of so many policies and practices that were contrary to Treeview's corporate philosophies and values. And he remembered that macabre guillotine.

After they complete their initial work on the values themselves, I would like the members of the task force—along with others—to begin an in-depth analysis of our company policies and written procedures. I want us to identify those practices that are out of sync with our stated values and consider all appropriate changes.

The task force will begin by examining all of our policies and practices that have to do with people. This will include reviewing our work rules, discipline procedures and other practices which I have come to believe may be the most out of sync with the values we so proudly display on walls everywhere.

Describing how the task team would also examine Treeview's performance appraisal process, Bill shifted to the subject of accountability.

Starting today, everyone at Treeview will also be held to a higher level of accountability. Specifically, that means we will all be evaluated not only on hard measures such as production results, but also on soft measures such as how we work with everyone from customers to colleagues.

Our current job descriptions identify the specific functions we perform. But it is our values that describe <u>how</u> we should perform those functions. Practicing our shared values is an important part of every employee's job.

Bill made it very clear that everyone would now be rated on value-driven performance and that the process would begin with management evaluations.

As he spoke, Bill noticed that Sally Wilson and Jim Gould, both of the client services department, shared a smile. Deep inside, he knew that Clarence was smiling, too.

With growing confidence and a new-found sensitivity, the CEO addressed an integral component of organizational accountability: measuring employee perceptions. He recalled a climate survey that had been handled secretly. Realizing that nothing substantive had been done with the data, he committed to the assembly that, this time, things would be different.

We'll also put together a separate task force to take a fresh look at the results of the climate survey that was done six months ago. Each of you has a meaningful viewpoint regarding how well we are or are not walking our talk. It's important, first, that we know what those perceptions are and, second, that we use that information to help shape the Treeview that we all envision.

Bill concluded these comments by suggesting that employee perceptions were as important—if not more important—than any other performance and accountability data that Treeview could collect. He guaranteed that employees would not only have similar feedback opportunities in the future, but also would be involved in helping the company determine exactly what the feedback meant.

Then, after suggesting that the changes he'd mentioned so far were only the beginning, he focused on yet another initiative.

Just this morning, I asked Carol Chandler, our vice president of human resources, to immediately begin working with the training staff to review our current educational format and curricula. Their ultimate task will be to ensure that ALL training activities specifically address and support our Treeview values.

At this point, Bill recalled a small paperweight on Karen Cooke's desk that read, "You Get What You Train For." And, he remembered Karen's third rule for walking the talk: *show them how*. "If we're going to expect our people to actually live our Treeview values," he had thought last night as he was preparing the speech, "we must show them how to do it." Bill determined that, from this day forward, training would become an activity through which people learned to *apply* values rather than merely explain them.

Pausing briefly to gaze into the now trusting eyes of his employees, Bill felt a twinge of guilt. The next subject he would address was particularly difficult for him. "How many times," he had wondered last evening, "have I been in meetings where our values were right there hanging on the wall? And, how many times have I neglected to include them in the decision-making process?" The number, he regretfully concluded, was too high to count. He had to assume that managers and supervisors had developed the same habit. He knew how easy it was to fall into this trap. Climbing out would be much tougher.

I believe that the true purpose of our value statements is to guide both our behaviors and our decisions. To be sure, not every decision we make will perfectly align with our values, but we must avoid those decisions which directly conflict with them. Therefore, today, I publicly commit to you that all future decisions I'm involved with will be tested against our values before they are finalized.

Making walking the talk our number one priority is a good idea that rightfully must start at the top. The initial plans that I've outlined today are just a few of the things that you can expect of me. Ensuring that we walk our talk, however, is not my responsibility alone. It's something we must do together. And, just as you have expectations of me, you must also have expectations of each other.

Bill had finally come to understand what Clarence meant by the "combination" to the gold. It was a *combination* of things that must be done by a *combination* of people. And, as Willie LaRue had so aptly suggested in his game plan, it could only be achieved by "going for singles rather than home runs."

Because everyone at Treeview would be responsible for walking the talk, it was now appropriate for Bill to focus on how each employee group must contribute to the big picture he had described. He directed his next series of comments to managers, supervisors, and individual contributors, respectively.

My challenge for Treeview managers is easily described: lead your departments by the book. The book I refer to is our shared values. I further challenge you to do this not because you'll be held to a higher level of accountability, although that's certainly a compelling reason, but rather because it is the right thing to do.

You see, our company is a large organization made up of many departments and divisions. With few exceptions, one's department IS Treeview, and each employee will judge the credibility of my words today by what happens within his or her particular piece of the organization. Therefore, it's critical that managers ensure their departments are about what we say our company is about. In other words, it's not good enough to walk the talk just at the corporate level. It must be a reality at the department level as well.

Bill recalled how Karen Cooke's five rules for walking the talk exemplified the way managers should develop personal plans for making their departments models of value-driven behavior. He went on to explain how each manager's departmental role mirrored Bill's own role within the larger organization.

The classic functions of management such as planning, organizing, and controlling are essential for success, but aimless without a meaningful context. For you, as well as for me, and from now on, that context must be our values.

Many practices in our organization are not governed by policy or written procedure. Therefore, merely relying on policy change recommendations from a task force won't totally ensure that we are walking the talk. Each manager and department must pick up where the task force leaves off.

We have to examine the unwritten rules and practices that happen every day and find ways to make necessary adjustments. As you and your business units continually strive to improve productivity, be leery of quick-fix fads and instant solutions. In many ways, I believe we've fallen prey to the 'program of the year' syndrome. Maybe we've just been programmed to death, and it's time to return to the basics that have never outlived their usefulness to us: our shared values.

Looking straight into the face of Bob Burnett, a highly respected supervisor at Treeview, Bill recalled the challenges he, himself, had faced early in his career. He remembered the frustration of feeling caught in the middle: employees viewed him as management, management viewed him more as an employee, and he saw himself as both . . . and neither.

He concluded that rather than identifying which group supervisors belonged to, it was more important to provide them with the guidance and tools necessary to be successful in their often difficult jobs. And this, he realized, would involve overcoming tradition.

When it comes to living our values, there may be no role more critical than that of the first-line supervisor. Because employees have more regular contact with you than anyone else at Treeview, you have the greatest opportunity, and a very important responsibility, to walk the talk.

Some of you may have learned supervision according to the old 'my way or the highway' model. And you may feel that we're changing the rules of the game on you. Well, we are changing the rules, but we're changing them for everyone.

The reason is simple: yesterday's way of managing not only doesn't work with today's workforce, but it also won't carry us into tomorrow. Change, you see, is a fact of life. And when that change involves doing a better job of practicing what we believe, it has to be a change for the better.

Bill acknowledged that in many ways supervisors and managers already walked the talk. He was sure, however, that the consistent practice of values was far from a way of life at Treeview.

Early in my career when I was a department supervisor, I wished for a cookbook that would help me unlock the mysteries of managing people. Later in life—after years of futile searching—I concluded there was no such book. My friends, yesterday I discovered I was wrong. I found that book, and its title is 'Treeview Values.'

Bill also challenged all supervisors to follow the modified game plan of a semi-pro baseball player he met only once, but would never forget.

Act according to the values and, by all means, don't start pointing fingers or waiting for others to begin. Focus on many small actions rather than a few big ones. Treat everyone like a winner, make sure they get the information they need to do their jobs, and allow all employees to share in the success.

One pair of eyes widened in anticipation at this last comment. Bill saw Glenda Thompson, an accounting clerk who hoped to be promoted to supervisor within a few months. As she tilted her head to listen more intently, Bill hoped she shared his visions and was seeking ways to turn them into reality.

The majority of you who are neither managers nor supervisors may wonder what role you play in this effort. It is to you that I offer the greatest challenge of all. And that's to avoid the assumption that walking the talk is solely the responsibility of management. Because we're all stakeholders in the success of this organization, I ask each of you to share not only the vision, but also the responsibility for making it happen.

Bill was not oblivious to Treeview's history. He knew the audience had heard words like this before. Too often, employee expectations had been raised only to be shattered in the cold reality of non-delivery. Skepticism was to be expected. But skepticism, he had concluded, comes from an individual's belief that *someone else* is responsible for action. No one is skeptical of himself.

The task had become clear: make employees partners in the change effort and focus on their responsibilities as partners.

Yesterday I learned a valuable lesson from a person I've never met. That person is Mike O'Toole, a nonmanagement employee like many of you. Mike operates by a simple principle that was passed along to me. I'd now like to pass it along to you.

Mike believes that you earn the right to expect others to do things by first doing those things yourself. I believe Mike is right, and I believe he has unlocked the secret to walking the talk.

Bill described how that simple principle is at the heart of walking the talk. Values are lived, he suggested, when people take the initiative to live them.

To make sure Treeview is prepared to meet the challenges of the future, we absolutely must avoid 'you go first' thinking. If we wait for the other person to start, we lose control of our own destiny.

Vision without action is meaningless. Waiting is one thing we cannot afford to do.

Specifically, I ask each of you here today to do what I commit I will do: examine Treeview's shared values and ask yourself how you might contribute to their application.

What can you do to further trust and mutual respect? How can you help ensure a safe and efficient workplace? What can you do this afternoon to operate in a partnership fashion? Are there ways you can contribute to the welfare of our community, improve our relationships with customers, or make a positive difference in the quality of our products and services?

Each of us has an assigned responsibility and a significant opportunity to take control and make things happen. It's our individual behaviors and actions that together afford us the greatest opportunity to live our values and ensure our continued success.

Making walking the talk our top business priority will involve many types and degrees of change. As we embark on this exciting journey, I believe it's prudent to remind ourselves about change itself.

As he spoke, Bill recalled snapshots of that magical journey which had made him more sensitive to human tendencies. Acknowledging the natural resistance to change, he reminded his audience that the process is often slow and painful—requiring people to abandon the very habits that provide comfort and stability.

And then he closed by cautioning the audience against expecting perfection.

No company, including Treeview, can ever be totally in sync with its values. Humans are imperfect and so are the organizations they create. Our efforts to do a better job of living our values will undoubtedly come with flaws. But if we meet those flaws and occasional failures with both persistence and patience, we can unlock the fortune within Treeview. My fellow employees, it's time for all of us to <u>walk the talk.</u> I thank you all.

The applause that followed his last words told Bill that his message had been well-received and appreciated. As he gathered his notes and prepared to leave, he was surrounded by a handful of people who had come on stage to both offer their congratulations and express their gratitude. The CEO had planted a seed of optimism that employees from all levels and departments appeared ready to nurture and harvest. Even those few who reacted less than enthusiastically still acknowledged that this speech was somehow different than "the same old stuff."

"That was a fabulous speech," said the manager of maintenance who met the CEO as he exited the stage. "I know you've been worried about it for several weeks, but you really nailed it today."

"Thanks," replied Bill. "But I really can't take all the credit. I got a lot of help yesterday from a very wise person."

"Who is that?" asked the manager.

"Believe it or not, it was a janitor. His name is Clarence."

"Now there's a coincidence for you," replied the manager.

"What do you mean?"

"We used to have a janitor here named Clarence—a little guy with a gold pocket watch that chimed."

"That's him!" exclaimed the CEO. "Do you know where I can find him? I'd really like to thank him."

The manager responded to Bill's words with a blank stare.

"What's the matter?" asked the CEO.

"We can't be talking about the same person. The Clarence I'm referring to passed away two years ago."

Dumbfounded by the manager's reply, Bill left the stage and started for his office.

"It's not possible," he thought as he walked, "to meet a man who no longer exists. There is no elevator in the auditorium. And all that couldn't possibly have happened in just one minute." He was now sure that the journey he so vividly pictured never actually occurred.

More than anything else, Bill was saddened by the realization that there was no Clarence, for this was the image of a man he had come to know and respect.

"Congratulations," said Bill's assistant as he entered his office. "It was a very moving speech. I'm really excited about our future."

"Thank you, Maria. I appreciate that."

"By the way," continued the assistant, "I think someone left something for you. It's on your desk."

Bill quickly found the object Maria was referring to. There, sitting in the middle of his desk blotter, was a gold pocket watch. Just as he picked it up, it began to chime.

Epilogue

A message to the reader . . . from Clarence

I hope you enjoyed the journey I took with Bill Elby. But more important than that, I hope you got something out of it.

You see, this is not the story of just one organization named Treeview and one executive named Bill. It's really the story of all organizations, and its message is for all people who make those organizations work and grow every single day.

The places I took Bill to, and the people we met along the way, exist in every company. They may look a little different, but believe me, they are there. It's up to you to find them and learn from them.

Your company's talk may be different than Treeview's. And your way of walking that talk may be different than Karen Cooke's, Willie LaRue's, Mike O'Toole's, and Bill Elby's. But that doesn't matter. What does matter is that you find your own way to walk your talk—whatever way that might be.

Whether you're an individual contributor, a supervisor, a manager, or even a janitor, never forget that you are responsible for making it happen. Words to live by are just words, unless YOU live by them.

Finally, whenever you hear a chime, or a bell, or an alarm, I hope you'll think of me and my watch. That sound means it's time to move on . . . it's time to *walk the talk*!

Clarence

A Collection of Quotations
from
Walk The Talk

Words to live by are just words, unless you live by them. You have to walk the talk.

page 22

When you break a promise, more than the promise gets broken.

page 24

Values are the gold that's in each of us. They're the real fortune of our organization.

page 36

When we talk about values, we're just sitting on a fortune. The more we practice them, the more gold we set free.

page 40

Even a fortune can collect dust if you let it.

page 41

When you make a promise, you have to deliver.

page 42

We judge ourselves mostly by our intentions, but others judge us mostly by our actions.

page 54

People hear what we say, but they see what we do. And seeing is believing.

page 60

I'm not talking about bothering folks. I'm talking about bothering WITH folks.

page 65

Sometimes, no matter what we do,
we get our heads cut off.
And what goes around
does come around.

page 66

Programs usually fail for one of two
reasons. Either they're bad ideas
to begin with, or they're good ideas
that are handled poorly.

page 70

Good things happen
when you make sure that
good things HAPPEN.

page 78

The better the means,
the better the ends.

page 87

Do right by those who do right.

page 88

If you can't do it, don't say it.
And if you can't say it,
don't play it.

page 90

We can't do really big things every day. If we're really serious about walking the talk all the time, we have to focus on the small stuff.

page 96

You earn the right to expect others to do things by doing those things yourself.

page 100

It seems to me the real world isn't a place as much as it is a bunch of actions. It's whatever we do.... Our values only become our real world when we walk the talk.

page 101

The two most important questions we must answer together are: what are we going to do about tomorrow, and how do we begin preparing for that reality today?

page 116

If these values are important enough to publish, they're important enough to live by.

page 120

Our current job descriptions identify the specific functions we perform. But it is our values that describe how we should perform those functions.

page 123

The true purpose of our value statements is to guide both our behaviors and our decisions.

page 127

It's critical that managers ensure their departments are about what we say our company is about.

page 129

Vision without action is meaningless.

page 137

Our efforts to do a better job of living our values will undoubtedly come with flaws. But if we meet those flaws and occasional failures with both persistence and patience, we can unlock the fortune...

page 139

About the Authors

Eric L. Harvey

Publishing Experience

Eric L. Harvey, President and CEO of Performance Systems Corporation, is the author of numerous articles dealing with the "people side of business." Specializing in the human resource areas of discipline, performance appraisal, and dispute resolution, Eric has dedicated over 20 years to helping corporations bring their people practices "in sync" with their corporate visions and values. Articles by and about Eric Harvey have appeared in *The Wall Street Journal*, *Harvard Business Review*, *Business Week*, *Executive Excellence*, *Industry Week*, and *Management Review*. He is also the author of two other books, *Discipline Without Punishment* and the award winning *PEER REVIEW: The Complete Guide.*

Consulting and Management Experience

Eric Harvey's background is a practical blend of hands-on experience ranging from production supervisor to labor relations and training management positions with several major corporations including Champion International and Johnson & Johnson. He is co-founder of Performance Systems Corporation, a fifteen-year-old firm specializing in human resource consulting.

Innovator for Clients

As a nationally known and respected speaker, author, and educator, Eric has pioneered innovative new human resource technologies that have assisted organizations such as Exxon, Procter & Gamble, Shell Oil, AT&T, General Electric, American Airlines, and *The Washington Post* in translating good ideas about managing people into everyday practice.

Personal

Eric Harvey is a graduate of the University of Texas and has served as adjunct faculty member at both the University of Alabama and Trinity University in their graduate programs. He lives with his wife Nancy and their daughters Nicole and Erika in Highland Village, Texas.

Alexander D. Lucia

Professional Experience

Alexander D. Lucia is Executive Vice President of Performance Systems Corporation. Formerly with Ford Motor Company and American Medicorp, Al has held management positions in the areas of recruitment, salary administration, organizational planning, benefits, and labor relations. His twenty-year human resource history is highlighted with many successful management development and culture change initiatives for major corporations throughout the United States and Canada. His list of clients includes such notables as General Electric, Exxon, Amoco, and Martin Marietta.

Product Technology and Development

With Eric Harvey, Al Lucia has developed two of Performance Systems' most successful human resource technologies: POSITIVE DISCIPLINE® and PEER GRIEVANCE REVIEW.®

Diversified Perspective

Al Lucia has served at the corporate staff level, the divisional level, and the facility level. He has worked in domestic and international environments, in industrial and service sectors, with large and small organizations, and in union and non-union settings. He is equally at home with top-level management, mid-level management, supervisory, and non-management employees.

Personal

After receiving his bachelors degree in Business Administration from Drexel University in Philadelphia, Al did his graduate work in Industrial Relations at Temple University. He has three daughters—Lisa, Pamela and Tracy—and lives in Oxford, Pennsylvania, the home of Performance Systems' east coast operations.

Performance Systems Corporation is a management consulting firm specializing in helping organizations bring their people practices in sync with today's visions and values for tomorrow's successes. For more information about our innovative human resource systems and services, or **to order additional copies of *Walk The Talk*,** contact: